Laylokhon Akhmedova

Teaching Russian/Foreign Language and Literature in Uzbekistan

Laylokhon Akhmedova

Teaching Russian/Foreign Language and Literature in Uzbekistan

ScienciaScripts

Imprint

Any brand names and product names mentioned in this book are subject to trademark, brand or patent protection and are trademarks or registered trademarks of their respective holders. The use of brand names, product names, common names, trade names, product descriptions etc. even without a particular marking in this work is in no way to be construed to mean that such names may be regarded as unrestricted in respect of trademark and brand protection legislation and could thus be used by anyone.

Cover image: www.ingimage.com

This book is a translation from the original published under ISBN 978-620-2-19720-5.

Publisher:
Sciencia Scripts
is a trademark of
Dodo Books Indian Ocean Ltd. and OmniScriptum S.R.L publishing group

120 High Road, East Finchley, London, N2 9ED, United Kingdom
Str. Armeneasca 28/1, office 1, Chisinau MD-2012, Republic of Moldova, Europe
Printed at: see last page
ISBN: 978-620-8-03589-1

Copyright © Laylokhon Akhmedova
Copyright © 2024 Dodo Books Indian Ocean Ltd. and OmniScriptum S.R.L publishing group

Table of contents

TEACHING RUSSIAN LITERATURE IN SCHOOLS OF THE REPUBLIC OF UZBEKISTAN

The fundamental changes that have taken place in the sovereign Republic of Uzbekistan over the years of its independence have required a rethinking of the content of education and upbringing of the younger generation. The revision of the concept of literary education is conditioned by the new requirements of life and the needs and tasks facing modern society.

Art education and moral and aesthetic education based on national-cultural and universal values become the basis of humanization of secondary general education school. Literature as a discipline of emotional and figurative character is addressed first of all to a person, his mind, soul, his inner world, which is a powerful factor of influence on the formation of personality.

The school is called upon to orient the growing person in the culture accumulated by society over millennia of civilization and constantly created by it. At the same time, the school is obliged to promote the self-determination of the student's prevailing abilities, preparation for real participation in the life of society and an informed choice of profession.

For this purpose it is necessary to define the goals of each period of school literary education based on the age capabilities of the pupil and the leading type of activity. It should be noted that the stages of literary development do not coincide with the periods of education in a modern school.

The works of fiction included in the literature course for grades 5-9 of Uzbek schoolchildren are divided conventionally into three sections.

The first section is works for detailed study (or textual analysis) in class. They are placed under the headings of the program topics.

The second section is works for additional reading, also specified in the program. They expand students' understanding of the writer's work, allow them to talk about the direction and problems of his work, about his creative path. Reading of these works is obligatory, and the nature of the analysis is determined by the teacher depending on the plan for studying the topic.

The third section is works for independent extracurricular reading. It changes from year to year and is replenished in accordance with the development of literature (information about this is regularly published in the scientific and methodological journal of the Republic of Uzbekistan "Teaching Language and Literature", accompanied by methodological recommendations).

It should be noted that secondary general education schools in Uzbekistan provide instruction from grades 1-9 and are conditionally divided into three stages (Russian literature as an academic subject is studied from grade 5).

In elementary school (grades 1-4, first stage) they practice elementary ways of communication with a literary text, forming the first skills of analytical work with a work of fiction.

At the second stage of literary education (5-7 grades) the main task of education becomes the formation of the ability to see the difference between one writer and another, to understand the originality of the worldview and artistic style of the writer within the framework of the analysis of a separate work.

At the third stage of literary education (8-9 grades) it is necessary to reveal to pupils the laws of literature as a special kind of art. Therefore, the theory of literature and the moral-historical aspect of the study of verbal art are brought to the forefront, and the system of comparing literature with other kinds of art (painting, theater, cinema) becomes imperative.

Extracurricular reading creates the necessary prerequisites for studying literature in the classroom. For the teacher, extracurricular reading is the best way to test the effectiveness of teaching, the ability to transfer knowledge and skills acquired in the classroom, in the sphere of free communication with art.

The theory of literature in the current Russian literature program is associated with the specific study of artistic phenomena. The sequence of mastering theoretical and literary concepts is determined by induction: tropes, structure of a work of fiction, genera and genres of literature, artistic individuality of a writer, and, finally, historical poetics.

Thus, in all spheres of literary education (reading and analyzing a work, literary theory, extracurricular reading, literary creativity) it is necessary to avoid at different stages of development similar operations and stimulate the progressive movement of the student.

The process of literary education in the schools of the republic is carried out in a multinational cultural, historical and ethnic environment. In these conditions, in our opinion, it is necessary to pay attention to centuries-old Russian-Uzbek historical, cultural and literary interrelations, to the interaction of national cultures, the history of Russian culture and literature in Uzbekistan, which will undoubtedly influence the formation of patriotic feelings in students, their involvement in the current events.

The process of studying native and world (including Uzbek) literature is connected with the penetration of schoolchildren into the spiritual culture of the people, with the assimilation of universal ideas about the basic criteria of morality developed by mankind.

It is well known that the literary development of the student is directly related to the general development, the formation of worldview, the evolution of moral assessments and ideas.

Therefore, the task of the course of literature at school is to rely on the general development of the student and stimulate it, contributing to the growth of personality.

The general goal of literary education in secondary school is to familiarize students with the riches of native and world fiction, to develop their ability of aesthetic perception and appreciation of works of word art, to form their aesthetic tastes and needs, moral and value guidelines, to develop emotional and figurative speech of schoolchildren.

The general indicators of achieving the goal of literary education are: -readiness of students (versatility, systematicity, directionality of reading); formation of reading interests;

- depth of mastering the ideological and figurative content of the work;

- the level of mastery of knowledge of literary theory;

- quality of speech skills formed in the process of studying literature.

The content of literary education in secondary general education schools of the Republic of Uzbekistan is determined by the basic component defined by the State Educational Standard and the solution of specific tasks at each stage.

Works of Russian literature occupy a central place in the program. At the same time, pupils familiarize themselves with works of world literature (in translation), which creates prerequisites for the formation of ideas about the unity and diversity of world literature and the originality and uniqueness of Russian literature. For example, studying Russian, Uzbek folk and literary fairy tales, fairy tales of the peoples of the world, pupils comprehend the ethical notions of good and evil inherent in human beings in general, comprehend the artistic features of the language of fairy tales, their allegorical meaning.

Russian literature of the 19th century is presented in the program quite voluminously, which is due to its global significance. The works of this period provide great opportunities for students to comprehend various human characters, their national and universal content.

A significant place is given to the Russian literature of the 20th century, which has a great artistic and educational potential and presents thematic and genre diversity.

The program also contains oriental works reflecting the theme of the East in the works of Russian writers and poets (e.g. I.A. Bunin, S.A. Esenin, A.A. Akhmatova). These works make it possible to reveal the commonality of historical destinies of the peoples, their movement along the path of ethno-cultural understanding.

The program also reflects the Russian literature of Uzbekistan (works by Russian writers living in Uzbekistan and works by Uzbek writers and poets writing in Russian), represented by the names of A. Ivanov, N. Krasilnikov, S. Madaliev, A. Feinberg, R. Farhadi and others.

The content of the subject "Literature" includes works of fiction, essays on the life of writers and poets, information on the theory of literature, literary-critical and educational articles, commentaries, etc.

The program of studying Russian literature is built on concentric and chronological principles (in each class, starting from the literature of the past - to the modern one).

The conceptual principle allows to establish continuity in teaching (for example, the same writer is represented at each stage of education by different works with gradual complication of problems, system of images, genre-composition features of works, etc.), to take into account the age interests and opportunities of students.

The chronological principle does not exclude other principles of combining the studied works. For example, in grade 5 it is combined with genre and problem-thematic (oral folk art, literary fairy tales, fables).

Thus, as the experience of work with students during the qualifying pedagogical practice in secondary schools of general education of the Republic of Uzbekistan shows, the program of studying Russian literature, built on concentric and chronological principles, helps students to comprehend the process of development of literature, its close connection with life, the specificity of reflection of reality in the art form. In addition, this arrangement of literary material, in our opinion, creates optimal opportunities for the realization of intra-subject and inter-subject links, correlation of themes, images, genres of different literatures and other arts (painting, music, sculpture, theater, etc.).

TOWARD THE USE OF INFORMATION TECHNOLOGIES IN TEACHING FOREIGN LANGUAGES AT THE UNIVERSITY

REPUBLIC OF UZBEKISTAN

The birth of all educational systems in the world has always been predetermined and conditioned by socio-economic orders of society. The super task of all these systems is to give society an educated person who can think critically, be able to generate new ideas, think creatively, acquire and apply knowledge independently in practice, work competently with information (search, analyze, systematize, summarize, draw conclusions and make constructive proposals), be communicative, contactable in various social groups, be able to work together in different areas and situations, preventing or skillfully getting out of any conflict situations, independently and independently. That is why the inexhaustible source of true knowledge and age-old wisdom has always been and remains education, the accession to which gives a person freedom and realization of his talents and opportunities for success.

... In 1420 in Samarkand, the great scholar and state ruler Mirzo Ulugbek inaugurated the majestic building of the Registan Madrasah built under his leadership. Addressing the first lesson to his students he said: "Our studies, friendship with people, honoring the elders, paying attention to the young - all this has a specific goal: to make people good, so that the era of piety would come, and Maverannahr would become the true face of the earth, the center of knowledge and great faith" (1, 295). This goal is still key today, as it is inextricably linked to the need to fully improve the quality of teacher education in the independent Republic of Uzbekistan, to determine the priorities and prospects of its development in the conditions of modernization of the state and its integration into the world community. That is why the development of education as the most important sphere of human activity, which ensures the formation of the intellectual potential of society, remains one of the priority tasks of our state policy.

The current stage of socio-economic development of the republic is characterized by an ever wider informatization and computerization of its various spheres. A qualitatively new stage in the modernization of the educational system is the development and introduction of modern pedagogical and information-communication technologies in the educational process.

The modern world is fast-paced, and in these conditions the teacher should not only keep up with the progress, but also be ahead of it, using all available technical, information and communication, psychological means to solve educational and upbringing tasks. In our opinion, today it is no longer enough to simply master the material and retell it to students, the teacher is required to have a special energy based on his/her own conviction in the correctness of the ideas he/she presents. And in this case, we believe that an important condition for the effectiveness of the educational process is the active use of modern information technologies, which increase its attractiveness in the eyes of students.

Here *new opportunities* open up: reduction of time for search and access to necessary educational and scientific information by teachers and students; acceleration of updating the content of education by reducing the time of teachers for the development of new educational and methodological literature; release of additional time for students for individual independent work; acceleration in the achievement by students of the established requirements for the quality of education and others.

Information technologies provide students with a variety of modern teaching tools, which, in addition to traditional textbooks and notes, include computer-based training programs; electronic textbooks and teaching aids; computer-based testing and knowledge control systems; electronic reference books and encyclopedias; educational audio and video materials; information materials posted on the Internet.

In recent years, one of the actual innovations is the active use of interactive whiteboard as a means of increasing the intensification of the learning process due to interactivity, visibility and dynamism of material presentation. Interactive whiteboard opens new opportunities for improving the learning process, activates and makes creative independent and joint work of students and teacher. Local network and access to the Internet allows to use authentic materials. In addition, teachers create their own interactive aids, developing them in accordance with the approved program for subjects.

The listed means of information technologies in Uzbekistan are used in teaching foreign languages both directly in the process of classroom work and for independent work in preparation for practical and seminar classes, which, in our opinion, is the most effective in the process of applying this type of innovative technologies.

An equally significant model of learning in modern conditions is the interactive approach as an alternative to the traditional system of learning, when the learner mechanically assimilated the knowledge put into it. Interactive provides students with an opportunity for *self-expression and self-realization,* independent search for knowledge on a particular discipline. The essence of interactive learning lies in the most versatile nature of students' activities, namely: *physical* (students change their workplace, talk, listen, write, do some creative work), *social* (discuss, ask questions and answer them, share impressions, experience of their own socialization) and *information and cognitive* activities (learn, study, independently find the necessary *information*, make reports, etc.).

What does the use of information technologies and interactive approach in the learning process ultimately bring to the student, the microgroup, and the teacher? To the *student*: it increases motivation, teaches to think unconventionally, teaches to enter into partnership relations, teaches tolerance, benevolence, tact; to the *microgroup*: it teaches to justify their positions, forms value-oriented unity of the group, teaches to resolve conflict situations and find compromise, forms life values; to the *teacher*: it forms trusting relations with students, activates non-standard attitude to the organization of the educational process, promotes multidimensional presentation of the material.

We believe that the integration of interactive information technologies into the process of teaching foreign languages is not a tribute to fashion, but an urgent need for teachers who not only seek to optimize the learning process, but also to make it modern, effective and motivated.

In conclusion, let us emphasize that innovation processes cannot and should not be finite. Each new day puts forward new requirements to the process of education. Therefore, our task is to rely on all previous experience of pedagogical thought development, constantly moving forward, scientifically substantiating and introducing new technologies of teaching and education of students and providing all subjects of the educational process with the opportunity to grow their creative innovative potential.

LITERATURE

1. Andriyanova V.I. Formation of students' abilities of self-expression and self-realization as basic qualities of personality - the dictates of time / Scientific and methodological manual for teachers and professors. - Tashkent, 2012.

ON THE STATE EDUCATIONAL STANDARD FOR FOREIGN LANGUAGES OF THE CONTINUOUS EDUCATION SYSTEM OF THE REPUBLIC OF UZBEKISTAN

The integration of our country into the international community, the development of science and technology require that the young generation should have a good command of several foreign languages in order to function competitively in a multicultural world. Knowledge of a foreign language is one of the components of professional competence of specialists of any profile. The Decree of the President of the Republic of Uzbekistan I.A. Karimov "On measures to further improve the system of foreign language learning" dated December 10, 2012 once again confirms the importance of modernization and renewal in the upbringing of an educated and intellectually advanced generation, which is the most important value and a decisive force in the development of a democratic society.

The resolution notes, "... an analysis of the current system of organizing foreign language learning shows that educational standards, curricula and textbooks do not fully meet modern requirements, especially with regard to the use of advanced information and media technologies. Teaching is carried out mainly by traditional methods. The organization of the continuity of foreign language learning at all levels of the education system requires further improvement" (1).

Hence, the relevance of developing state educational standards for ILE in the system of continuing education of the Republic of Uzbekistan.

When developing state educational standards, it was necessary to ensure the introduction of international standards for teaching foreign language into the educational system of the Republic of Uzbekistan. The document of the Council of Europe "Common European

Framework of Reference for Languages: Learning, Teaching, Assessment" is one of such universally recognized international standards. Taking into account some provisions of this document, the present State Educational Standard on Foreign Language Learning in the System of Continuing Education of the Republic of Uzbekistan has been developed.

The fundamental normative-legislative documents for the compilation of the state educational standard on IEL for all levels of education (general secondary, specialized secondary and higher education) of the Republic of Uzbekistan are: The Constitution of the Republic of Uzbekistan; the UN Convention on the Rights of the Child; the laws of the Republic of Uzbekistan "On Education", "National Program on Personnel Training"; the Decree of the President of the Republic of Uzbekistan I.A. Karimov from December 10, 2012 № 1875 "On measures for further improvement of the system of foreign language learning".

The state educational standard for continuous, successive teaching of the language provides for the study of the language at the following levels:

1.   Elementary Education - Grades 1 - 4.

2.   Secondary Education - Grades 5-9.

3.   Academic high schools and vocational colleges.

4.   Higher education institution (bachelor's, master's degree).

Thus, the principle of continuous and successive language general secondary, specialized secondary and vocational, higher education in the field of language learning is realized, which corresponds to the needs of the individual and society and implies the formation of communicative competence of graduates of educational institutions of the Republic of Uzbekistan.

The study of foreign language in the system of continuous education in Uzbekistan on the basis of the State Educational Standards is carried out in the following order:

Level of education	Graduates	CEFR level	Title levels
General secondary education	Graduates of elementary schools	A 1	Basic elementary level of language proficiency
	9th grade graduates	A 2	Basic level of language proficiency
	Graduates of the 9th grade of state general education specialized schools with advanced study of foreign languages	A 2+	Basic enhanced level of language proficiency
Secondary specialized professional education	Graduates of the academic lyceum of non-language profile	B 1	Level of independent elementary language proficiency
	Graduates of vocational colleges		
	Graduates of academic lyceums of language profile - second language		
	Graduates of academic lyceums with a language profile	B 1+	Level of independent enhanced language proficiency
	Bachelor's degree graduates of non-language faculties of higher education institutions	B 2	Independent language proficiency level
Higher education	Bachelor's degree graduates of language faculties of higher education institutions - second language		
	Master's degree graduates of non-language faculties of higher education		

institutions		
Bachelor's degree graduates of language faculties of higher education institutions	C 1	Level of professional primary language proficiency
Master's degree graduates of language faculties of higher education institutions		

The CEFR levels of proficiency in IFL according to the CEFR are summarized as follows:

A1. I understand and can use in speech familiar phrases and expressions necessary to perform specific tasks. I can introduce myself/introduce others, ask/answer questions about residence, acquaintances, property. I can participate in a simple conversation if the other person speaks slowly and clearly and is willing to help.

A2. I understand individual sentences and frequently occurring expressions related to basic spheres of life (e.g. basic information about myself and my family members, shopping, getting a job, etc.).

A2+. I can perform tasks related to simple exchange of information on familiar or everyday topics. In simple terms, I can talk about myself, my family and friends, and describe basic aspects of everyday life.

81. I understand the main ideas of clear messages made in a literary language on various topics that typically arise in work, study, leisure, etc. I am able to communicate in most situations that may arise during a stay in the country of the target language.

B1+. I can compose a coherent message on topics I know or am particularly interested in. I can describe impressions, events, hopes, aspirations, state and justify my opinion and plans for the future.

82. I can understand the general content of complex texts on abstract and concrete topics, including highly specialized texts. I speak quickly and spontaneously enough to communicate with native speakers on a regular basis without difficulty for either party. I am able to make clear, detailed presentations on various topics and present my view on the main problem, show the advantages and disadvantages of different opinions.

83. I can understand complex texts on various subjects and recognize hidden meanings. I speak spontaneously at a fast pace without difficulty in selecting words and expressions. I use language flexibly and effectively to communicate in scientific and professional activities. I can create precise, detailed, well-organized messages on complex topics, demonstrating mastery of models of text organization.

The state educational standard is based on communicative-activist, personality-oriented, integrative and competence-based approaches to language teaching.

The **communicative-activistic approach** has a developmental, functional and communicative character of teaching, which contributes to the increase of cognitive activity in learning. This approach is focused on the formation of students' ability and need for reflection, self-development and self-actualization. This is based on the integration of different fields of knowledge into the learning process, organization of the learning process as a process of intercultural communication, cooperation between the learner and the learner as equal participants of the learning process, application of interactive forms of learning; development of learners' independence in acquiring new linguistic and socio-cultural knowledge and practical skills.

Personality-oriented approach to teaching ELL consists in the development of teaching content based not only on scientific knowledge, but also on metacognition (techniques and methods of cognition) and special forms of interaction between participants in the educational process (students, teachers, parents). This approach implies special procedures for tracking the nature and direction of a student's development, creating favorable conditions for the formation of his/her individuality, and determining the dynamics of the child's development in comparison with himself/herself rather than with others.

The **integrative approach to teaching ILE** implies the proportional use in the learning process of the material selected from different spheres of students' activity (adaptation, personal-relevant, general intellectual and professional); a balanced ratio of language and speech material; complex and mutual formation of the required and actually achievable levels of speech readiness in the four main types of speech activity.

The competency-based approach to language teaching is aimed at achieving certain results and acquiring meaningful competencies. Competences are formed in the process of activity for the sake of future professional activity. The learning process under this approach is the acquisition of knowledge, skills, abilities, skills and experience of activity in order to achieve professionally and socially significant competencies in independent, educational and cognitive, social and cultural and leisure spheres of activity.

In structural terms, the State educational standard for the foreign language for all levels of education consists of the goal and objectives of studying the subject; the content of education; requirements for the mandatory level of preparedness of graduates of educational institutions at all levels of education.

The **aim of teaching IEL** at all levels of education is to form foreign language communicative competence of students for functioning in a multicultural world in everyday, scientific and professional spheres.

Competence is a sum of knowledge, skills and personal qualities that allow to perform various actions, conditioned by specific motives and goals set, including the participant of communication.

Foreign-language communicative competence is "the ability and real readiness to carry out foreign-language communication with native speakers, as well as familiarization of pupils with the culture of the country/countries of the target language, better understanding of the culture of their own country, ability to represent it in the process of communication" (2).

The objectives of foreign language learning include the acquisition of the following competencies:

Linguistic competence, which implies knowledge of language material (phonetics, vocabulary, grammar) and mastery of speech activities (listening, speaking, reading, writing) to a sufficient extent to communicate with representatives of the cultures of the target language.

Sociolinguistic competence, which allows choosing the right linguistic form and mode of expression depending on the situation, communicative purpose and intention of the speaker. Sociolinguistic competence includes **sociocultural competence**, which provides the ability to recognize the national characteristics of the country of the target language and behave accordingly in situations of foreign language communication and in communication with native speakers.

Pragmatic competence, which ensures the ability to communicate in accordance with the development of the communicative situation in the language and strategies that contribute to the effectiveness of communication, such as strategies of interruption, clarification, compensation in situations of difficult communication. In these standards, **discourse** competence is included in the pragmatic **competence**. It develops the ability to connect ideas coherently, using appropriate linguistic means in oral and written communication, as well as the ability to understand and interpret linguistic signals in coherent oral speech or in writing (2).

The **content of training** is presented in the form of a set of subject topics included in the basic curricula of general secondary, specialized secondary and higher education. The teaching material at all levels of education ensures continuity, consistency and cyclicality of education.

The continuity of learning is ensured by taking into account the intra-subject links in the formation of all components of foreign language communicative competence. Consistency consists in the fact that the newly studied material is based on the material mastered by students earlier. Cyclicality manifests itself in the fact that a certain amount of material is mastered within a cycle - a certain number of lessons/sessions. Each of such cycles is based on the stage-by-stage development of this or that skill and ability for each type of speech activity. All cycles are complete independent periods of learning, aimed at solving specific tasks to achieve the overall goal of acquiring the language skills.

The **requirements for the level of graduates' proficiency in** the **foreign** language are developed in accordance with the content of training and continuity at the levels of general secondary, specialized secondary and higher education and are presented in the form of descriptors (can do), forming language skills and abilities, and guidelines on grammar, vocabulary, phonetics and orthography as necessary. The language skills and abilities descriptors are interlinked and borrowed from the Common European Framework of Reference for Languages to ensure consistency with international standards. The descriptors are presented in an accessible form for learners, teachers and other stakeholders to understand.

Thus, in conclusion, it should be noted that on May 8, 2013, the Cabinet of Ministers of the

Republic of Uzbekistan Decree No. 124 "On Approval of the State Educational Standard on Foreign Languages of the Continuing Education System" approved the State Educational Standard of the Continuing Education System "Requirements for the level of preparedness of graduates of all levels of education in foreign languages".

LITERATURE

1.   Decree of the President of the Republic of Uzbekistan № 1875 "On measures to further improve the system of learning foreign languages" from 10.12.2012.

2.   A Common European Framework of Reference for Languages: Learning, Teaching, Assessment. - Common European Framework of Reference for Languages: Learning, Teaching, Assessment. - http://www.linguanet.ru. - (Russian translation of Moscow State Linguistic University). - 2003 г.

THE ROLE OF THE FIRST PRESIDENT ISLAM KARIMOV IN MODERNIZING THE EDUCATION SYSTEM IN UZBEKISTAN

Dedicated to the memory of the First President of the Republic of Uzbekistan

Islam Karimov

"If a person does not dream of the future, then know, this person has lost something. People should live and strive for high goals, not only in dreams, but also in real life, they should soar, achieve great victories, improve themselves". I.A. Karimov.

Every day we have witnessed high professionalism and responsibility, human decency and simplicity, self-control and determination - everything that our First President Islam Abduganievich Karimov - the founder of independent Uzbekistan, who devoted his whole life to his native country, the well-being of the people and prosperity of our independent country - did[1].

The role of the first head of our state can be talked about not only on the scale of the republic, but also the world. The talented initiator and wise leader left an indelible mark in the history of our country, taught us to love and be proud of our Motherland, brought Uzbekistan to the international level, making it famous throughout the world. Thanks to his far-sighted wise policy, courage and determination, Uzbekistan has turned into a country where peace, tranquility and stability reign, where representatives of various nationalities and confessions live in friendship and harmony.

The people of Uzbekistan rightfully associate the outstanding achievements of the years of independence with the name and activities of Islam Karimov. He is the initiator and leader of

---

1 On March 24, 1990, the post of President was established for the first time in the history of Uzbekistan. On December 29, 1991, I.A. Karimov was elected President of the Republic of Uzbekistan in a nationwide alternative election.

the historic transformations in the country. Under his direct leadership, the following were developed and implemented: a programme for the independent development of the country, the Constitution of the Republic of Uzbekistan, which meets all democratic requirements and international criteria; a new programme of State and social construction, which provides for the implementation of the principles of harmonizing the interests of the State, society and the individual; a model of economic development, recognized far beyond the borders of Uzbekistan, based on the well-known five principles of de-ideologizing e

It was he who raised to the level of state policy the respectful attitude to the spiritual values of the people, the revival, preservation and development of religion, traditions and customs, and the invaluable historical heritage; who made a major contribution to enhancing the authority, respect and support for Uzbekistan in the international arena; who made a significant contribution to the formation and introduction into public consciousness of the foundations of a national ideology based on universal and national values and traditions;

The great achievements achieved thanks to the wise and far-sighted policy of the First President Islam Karimov cannot be counted. They are in everything: in every sphere, at every step.

I would like to emphasize that Islam Karimov is the author of a number of books included in the multi-volume collection of essays devoted to topical issues. Among them: "Uzbekistan: its own path of renewal and progress", "Uzbekistan on the path of deepening economic reforms", "Uzbekistan on the threshold of the 21st century: threats to security, conditions and guarantees of progress", "The Motherland is sacred for everyone", "There is no future without historical memory", "Uzbekistan aspiring to the 21st century", "High spirituality is an invincible force", "The global financial and economic crisis, ways and measures to overcome it in the conditions of Uzbekistan" and others. He is also the author of numerous articles and reports. Many works of our First President have been translated into English, French, Spanish, German, Indian, Chinese, Arabic and other languages of the world.

I.A. Karimov gives an important place in his works to the issues of education and upbringing, emphasizing that "... a new democratic concept of education is to be developed and implemented, in which national, historical and cultural traditions, moral experience of Uzbek and other peoples living in the territory of the republic would be organically included in the system of education and upbringing" [9]. [9].

Speaking of the education of youth and its role in the prosperity of our homeland, he notes that " .... to achieve the noble goals of the nation

The future of Uzbekistan, the country's prosperity and well-being, the place it will occupy in the world community in the twenty-first century - all this depends, first of all, on the new generation, on how our children will grow up.... Our goal is to create the necessary opportunities and conditions for our children to grow up not only physically and spiritually healthy, but also comprehensively and harmoniously developed people with the most modern intellectual knowledge, people who fully meet the requirements of the twenty-first century, in which they will have to live and work". [12].

It is impossible not to agree with this thought. Our country needs intelligent and educated people. Let us remember the wise thought of the French writer Victor Hugo: "The greatness of a nation is not measured by its numbers, just as the greatness of a man is not measured by his height; the only measure is his mental development and his moral level" [18]. [18].

In Uzbekistan, over the years of independence, the main priority of the state policy has become the care for the upbringing of a developed young generation - physically healthy and spiritually mature, intellectually rich, possessing not only versatile knowledge, but also able to think independently and boldly look into the future.

The Constitution of the Republic of Uzbekistan enshrines the provision that everyone has the right to education, with the state guaranteeing free general education [1]. The beginning of a new stage of deep reforms in this most important sphere was the adoption of the Law "On Education" on August 29, 1997 on the initiative of the First President Islam Karimov [2] and the "National Program on Personnel Training" [2] [2] and the "National Program on Personnel Training" [3], which, according to international experts, has no analogues in terms of its significance, scope and objectives.

Over the years of independence, Uzbekistan has produced a truly versatile, gifted, talented, highly educated and intellectually advanced young generation. Today, the country's educational institutions are producing socially active, well-rounded and independently thinking individuals with their own views, a firm civic position and the right to choose. The new generation of purposeful young men and women have at least two or three professions, foreign languages, information technologies and modern knowledge. They are ready to compete on equal terms with their peers from developed countries. All this is the result of the tremendous work that has been carried out under the leadership of the First President of the Republic of Uzbekistan.

Islam Karimov loved the younger generation in a fatherly way and created all conditions for its harmonious development. He believed in and placed great hopes on the youth, considering them the biggest pillar, one could say invaluable potential, the driving force of today and tomorrow.

The International Conference held on the initiative of the First President on February 16-17, 2012 in Tashkent city "Training of educated and intellectually advanced generation as the most important condition for sustainable development and modernization of the country" confirms the abovementioned. This conference was held with the aim of broad familiarization of the international community with the accumulated experience and results of reforms in the field of education in Uzbekistan, the role of the state in training a highly educated and intellectually advanced generation.

The international conference was attended by about 1000 participants, including 270 representatives from 48 countries of the world and 8 international organizations and educational foundations. An important place in the work of the international conference was occupied by the report of Mr. I. Karimov. Karimov, which outlined the main goals and objectives, the essence and content of the Program of reforming the education system in Uzbekistan, training an educated and intellectually advanced generation. Speaking at the opening of the International Conference, the President emphasized: "Today there is no need to prove that the 21st century is widely recognized as the century of globalization and erasure of borders, information and communication technologies and the Internet, the century of ever-increasing competition in the global space and the world market. In these conditions, the state that has among its main priorities always the growth of investments and investments in human capital, training of educated and intellectually developed generation, which is the most important value in the modern world and a decisive force in achieving the goals of democratic development, modernization and renewal, can declare itself" [13]. [13].

It was emphasized at the conference that the Program adopted in 1997, called the National Program on Personnel Training, is an integral part of Uzbekistan's own "Uzbek model" of economic and political reforms, based on the step-by-step, evolutionary principle of building a new society in the country.

The President noted that our country attaches great importance to education and upbringing along with education. In this regard, he said: "Only people who realize the need for harmony of national and universal values, who have modern knowledge, intellectual potential and advanced technologies, can achieve the set strategic development goals. The main principles of reforming the education system should be.... formation in students of the priority of universal values, high spirituality, culture and creative thinking; organic unity of education with national history, folk traditions and customs, respect for the history and culture of other peoples" [13]. [13].

It can be stated with certainty (ed. personally participated in the work of this conference) that the conference allowed to exchange experience on such issues of the education system as the development of general secondary education, increasing the effectiveness of specialized secondary vocational education and strengthening its connection with the labor market, the development of higher education, the introduction of information and communication technologies in the educational process, strengthening and continuous interaction between higher education and science, the role of culture in the process of education, the role of culture in the development of the educational process, and the development of the educational system.

It is also worth mentioning the fact that with independence our country gained the opportunity to communicate freely with foreign countries. Therefore, the study of foreign languages and new information technologies has become an important task.

The opinion of psychologists and sociolinguists on this problem boils down to the fact that knowledge of any non-native language helps the individual to understand more deeply the native language, which remains an unshakable foundation for mastering any other language.

We agree with this statement, as the prestige of the mother tongue should not negatively influence the learning of other languages. A person who does not speak another language besides his/her mother tongue remains confined exclusively in one culture. That is why Chingiz Aitmatov's conviction that the wonderful world of literature and culture should be open to everyone and the main condition for this is the knowledge of not only the native language, but also other languages ... is wise and fair" [15]. [15].

In our opinion, knowledge of a foreign language is one of the components of professional competence of specialists of any profile. Decree of the First President of the Republic of Uzbekistan Islam Karimov "On measures to further improve the system of foreign language learning" dated December 10, 2012 (PP № 1875) once again confirms the importance of studying and raising the status of a foreign language in society, changing the socio-cultural context of learning languages of international communication, as the priority of language education is associated with the role of language in the life of society: language is a means of knowledge and communication, development and education, impact and self-actualization.

The Resolution notes, "... an analysis of the current system of organizing foreign language learning shows that educational standards, curricula and textbooks do not fully meet modern requirements, especially with regard to the use of advanced information and pedagogical technologies. Teaching is conducted mainly by traditional methods. The organization of continuity of foreign language learning at all levels of the education system requires further improvement..." *[4]*. [4].

What exactly has been done so far to improve the foreign language learning system in Uzbekistan?

In light of the implementation of this Resolution, the scientists of our country, with the participation of leading foreign training centers, international experts and specialists in the relevant foreign languages, based on the document of the Council of Europe "Common European Framework of Reference: Learning, Teaching, and Assessment" (CEFR - Common European Framework of Reference: Learning, Teaching, Assessment) [17] have developed the State Educational Standard of the Continuing Education System of the Republic of

Uzbekistan "Requirements for the level of proficiency of graduates of all levels of education in foreign languages", providing specific criteria for the level of knowledge of foreign languages at each level of education [17], the State Educational Standard of the Continuing Education System of the Republic of Uzbekistan "Requirements for the level of preparedness of graduates of all levels of education in foreign languages" was developed, providing specific criteria for the level of knowledge of foreign languages at each level of education. The State Educational Standard of the Continuing Education System of the Republic of Uzbekistan was approved by the Resolution of the Cabinet of Ministers of the Republic of Uzbekistan on May 8, 2013 [7].

On the basis of this standard, control and measurement parameters for state certification, curricula for foreign languages (English, French, German and others) have been developed taking into account the specifics of the educational institution and approved by the relevant orders of the ministries.

Further, since the 2013-2014 academic year, the study of foreign languages on the basis of the developed state educational standards and programs has been gradually introduced throughout the country from the first grade in general education schools. Teaching foreign languages to students in the first grades of general education schools is conducted in the form of game classes and conversation lessons, and in the second grades - mastering the alphabet, studying grammar and reading.

In higher education institutions, the teaching of certain specialized subjects, particularly in technical, medical and international specialties, is conducted in foreign languages.

Also, in order to implement the tasks set out in PP No. 1875, the Department for Assessment of Foreign Language Proficiency and Knowledge was established as part of the State Testing Center under the Cabinet of Ministers. It has developed and implemented the National Test

System for assessing the level of knowledge of foreign languages, taking into account the requirements of internationally recognized standards, and organized testing of applicants on a paid basis (including remotely: materials necessary for independent preparation of applicants for testing are available on the Internet) to determine the level of their knowledge and mastery of a foreign language with the issuance of the appropriate qualification certificate of state sample.

In addition, since the 2015/2016 academic year, foreign language has been introduced in the block of entrance exams (testing) to all higher education institutions.

Teachers and teachers of foreign languages are paid monthly supplements to their tariff rates in the amount of: 30% - in educational institutions located in rural areas; 15% - in other educational institutions (in the presence of a state-issued qualification certificate).

Taking into account the interests and hobbies of children and young people, television broadcasts, including local television channels, have been organized to teach children and adolescents foreign languages; popular science and educational programmes on the history and culture of other peoples and on the development of world science and technology; and foreign feature and animated films with subtitles in Uzbek.

In addition, access of educational institutions to international educational resources through ZiyoNet, saturation of its resource center with multimedia resources, educational applications for personal computers and mobile devices, as well as publication of educational and fiction literature, specialized illustrated newspapers and magazines in English, opening of special columns and supplements to them were increased.

Cooperation in the field of foreign language teaching with foreign educational institutions and embassies has also been effective and efficient. As a result of effective cooperation with a number of embassies, cultural centers of France, the United States, Germany, Spain, China, Italy, Japan, Poland, Egypt and South Korea to fulfill the tasks outlined in Resolution No. 1875, repeated training seminars, short-term professional development courses for foreign language teachers working in the system of continuing education, trips of English language teachers to leading educational institutions - British institutes - London Metropolitan and Norwich Institute of Linguistic and Cultural Studies - were held.

It is not insignificant that the government of Uzbekistan has established a new electronic scientific and methodological journal and Internet portal "Foreign Languages in Uzbekistan" (www.fledu.uz), designed to promote the development of domestic foreign language teaching methodology. They were formed by the Resolution of the Cabinet of Ministers No. 283 dated October 16, 2013 [8].

The e-journal publishes articles on achievements in the field of theory and methodology of foreign language teaching, as well as the most interesting articles from the work experience of practicing teachers. The e-journal and the Internet portal cover theoretical and methodological problems of foreign language learning, the results of the introduction of modern innovative methods of teaching foreign languages, tell about cultural ties between nations, etc. The e-journal and the Internet portal are also published.

It is interesting to note that the editorial board of the Internet portal and electronic scientific and methodological journal "Foreign Languages in Uzbekistan" in order to implement the resolution of the First President of the Republic of Uzbekistan № PP-1875 and the Cabinet of Ministers of the Republic of Uzbekistan № 283 and to discuss the most pressing issues of foreign language teaching methodology in the system of continuous education, taking into account the experience of other countries of the world, the problems of improving the quality of education and mechanisms to ensure its provision annually holds national and international conferences and seminars.

We believe that it is certainly important that every year on December 10 in the leading universities of our republic a scientific-practical conference dedicated to the anniversary of the adoption of the Decree of the First President of the Republic of Uzbekistan Islam Karimov "On measures to further improve the system of learning foreign languages" is held, where the results of work are summarized and new prospects for the implementation of all the tasks outlined in the Decree are outlined.

It should be noted that the process of implementing all the measures specified in the Decision of the First President of the Republic of Uzbekistan Islam Karimov "On measures to further improve the foreign language learning system" is continuing.

The position of our First President on modernization of the education system is also expressed in the resolution "On measures to improve the activities of the Uzbek State University of World Languages", signed on May 23, 2013 № PP - 1971, which notes that in order to ensure the implementation of measures to further develop the study of foreign languages, increase the level and quality of training of highly qualified teachers of foreign languages for secondary schools, vocational colleges and academic lyceums, higher education institutions, as well as to improve the quality of teaching of foreign languages in the country.

Thus, the "Republican Scientific and Practical Center for the Development of Innovative Methods of Teaching Foreign Languages" (hereinafter referred to as the Center), which includes a number of departments and groups for foreign language learning, was established at UzSUMYA. The purpose of the Center is to organize training of highly qualified teachers of foreign languages for secondary schools, vocational colleges, academic lyceums and higher educational institutions, knowing innovative educational technologies of teaching foreign languages; introduction of modern methods of teaching foreign languages, taking into account the study of international experience in all educational institutions of the system of continuous education, as well as institutions of advanced training and retraining of personnel

Retraining and professional development of management and pedagogical staff of higher educational institutions is also an important sector of education, and it was not left without attention of the First Head of our state. On June 12, 2015, I. Karimov signed a decree "On measures to further improve the system of retraining and professional development of managerial and pedagogical staff of higher educational institutions" [6]. [6].

The document was adopted in order to radically improve the quality of training of highly qualified specialists on the basis of continuous growth of professional level and qualification of the teaching staff of higher education institutions, introduction of an improved system of their regular retraining in accordance with modern requirements. The Decree defines 15 leading higher education institutions of our country as Basic Higher Education Institutions for the organization of retraining and professional development of leading and teaching staff of higher education institutions in the areas of retraining.

I. Karimov firmly believes that the path to the human soul begins with upbringing and education, and therefore in all his speeches he speaks with reverence about the noble work of teachers and mentors: "A teacher is a noble person whose vocation is to bring goodness and knowledge, to awaken a sense of humanism in young hearts, to teach the real science of life" [14]. [14]. On the initiative of Islam Karimov, the "Day of Teachers and Mentors" was established, which became one of the national holidays in the country.

In our opinion, the establishment of October 1 in our country as the "Day of Teachers and Mentors" - a wonderful holiday, declaring it a day off is a rare example in the world and a vivid confirmation of deep respect for us teachers, professors, mentors, educators on the part of the state, the whole nation and personal reverence of the First President. Here is the recommendation on this issue of the participants of the International Conference "Training of educated and intellectually advanced generation - as the most important condition for sustainable development and modernization of the country", held in Tashkent on February 16-17, 2012: " ... . it is necessary to study the possibility of introducing, for example

Uzbekistan, the "Day of Teachers and Mentors" as a national holiday, which will serve to confirm the public recognition and the role of teachers' work in the formation and education of a harmoniously developed personality."" [13].

Thus, the First President of our country created an absolutely new system of education, made great efforts for its implementation, setting before education the task of forming the intellectual, creative and spiritual potential of students in the conditions of multilingualism, and, in our opinion, it is the word, language, culture that contributes to its solution. Therefore, more than five and a half centuries ago, the great poet Alisher Navoi expressed a cherished dream, which sounds relevant today:

There's a lot I'd like to know--

O light of my dreams, in the name of creation. I would like to know the thoughts of all men and the languages of the whole creation [16].

It remains for all of us to follow this right path. And not to forget another prophetic thought expressed by the First President of the Republic of Uzbekistan Islam Karimov: "The decisive factor in the capabilities of every state, every nation is knowledge and education, intellectual and spiritual potential of people. Intellectual and spiritual and moral potential are the two wings of an enlightened person" [10]. It is safe to say that our people highly honor the merits of the great statesman Islam Karimov in achieving the independence of our homeland, ensuring a free and prosperous life, modernizing the education system and raising a harmoniously developed generation.

LITERATURE

1. Constitution of the Republic of Uzbekistan. - T., 1992.

2. Law of the Republic of Uzbekistan "On Education". - T., 1997.

3. National training program. - T., 1997.

4. Presidential Decision No. 1875 on measures to further improve the foreign language learning system, dated December 10, 2012.

5. Resolution of the President of the Republic of Uzbekistan I. Karimov № 1971 "On improving the activities of UzSUMYA" - T., 2013.

6. Decree of the President of the Republic of Uzbekistan "On measures to further improve the system of retraining and advanced training of managerial and pedagogical staff of higher educational institutions" dated June 12, 2015.

7. Resolution of the Cabinet of Ministers of the Republic of Uzbekistan No. 124 "State Educational Standard of Continuing Education System. Requirements for the level of preparedness of graduates of all levels of education in foreign languages". - T., 2013.

8. Resolution of the Cabinet of Ministers No. 283 of October 16, 2013 "On the formation of the Internet portal and professional electronic journal "Foreign Languages in Uzbekistan".

9. Karimov I.A. Uzbekistan: national independence, economy, politics, ideology. Speeches, articles, interviews. - T.: Uzbekistan, 1993. - C.73.

10. Karimov I.A. Speech by the President of Uzbekistan I.A. Karimov in May 2003 at the opening of the International Westminster University.

11. Karimov I.A. High spirituality - invincible power. - Tashkent: Ma'naviyat, 2008. - C.30.

12. Karimov I.A. Our main task is the further development of the country and increasing the welfare of the people: Report at the meeting of the Cabinet of Ministers of January 29, 2010. - Tashkent: Uzbekistan. - 2010. - C.67-68.

13. President Karimov's report at the opening of the International Conference on 16-17 February 2012 "Preparing an educated and intellectually advanced generation as the most important condition for sustainable development and modernization of the country" // Teacher of Uzbekistan. - February 17, 2012 - P. 1-3.

14. Address by President I.A.Karimov to teachers and mentors in honor of the "Day of Teachers and Mentors". - T., 2007.

15. Aitmatov Ch. It is necessary to know many languages // Russian language in the national school. - 1990. - № 7.

16. Navoi A. Selected Poems. - T., 1983.

17. Common European Framework of Reference for Languages: Learning, Teaching, Assessment. - Strasbourg, 1996. - Common European Framework of Reference for Languages: Learning, Teaching, Assessment / Russian translation of the Moscow State Linguistic University. - M., 2003.

18. https://www.inpearls.ru/

USE OF RCMCP TECHNOLOGY METHODS IN STUDYING THE STORY "BLACK COAT" BY L.S.PETRUSHEVSKAYA

The term "critical thinking" in various scientific studies has a completely different definition. According to J. Braus and D. Wood, critical thinking is a search for common sense and the ability to abandon one's own prejudices [2]. According to D. Halpern, critical thinking is "the use of such cognitive skills or strategies that increase the probability of obtaining the desired result, ... are characterized by deliberateness, logicality and purposefulness..... It is the type of thinking that is resorted to when solving problems, formulating conclusions, probabilistic evaluation, and making decisions. In doing so, the thinker uses skills that are reasonable and effective for the particular situation and type of problem being solved" [1]. In Lipman's works, critical thinking is defined as "skillful, responsible thinking that contributes to good judgment because it relies on criteria, is self-correcting, and is sensitive to context". D. Klooster defines the characteristics of critical thinking as follows: productive thinking, during which positive experience is formed from everything that happens to a person; argumentative, because convincing arguments allow making thoughtful decisions; multifaceted, because it is manifested in the ability to consider a phenomenon from different sides; individual, because it forms a personal culture of working with information; social, because work is carried out in pairs, groups; the main method of interaction is discussion [2].

In our opinion, critical thinking is the ability to synthesize and analyze information from the position of logic, the ability to pose new questions, develop a variety of arguments, and make independent, thoughtful decisions.

The purpose of the RWCT technology is to ensure the development of critical thinking through active (interactive) inclusion of students in the educational process. The use of this technology is focused on the development of thoughtful work with the text, with information and is a system of strategies that combine the techniques of learning work by types of learning activities depending on the nature of the text and the way of working with it.

We offer a description of a seminar class using the technology of development of critical thinking through reading and writing on the module "Innovative Educational Technologies", conducted with students of retraining and advanced training courses for teaching staff at the Republican Scientific and Practical Center for the Development of Innovative Methods for Teaching Foreign Languages (RNPCRIM) at the Uzbekistan State University of World Languages (UzSUMYA).

After listening to the lecture material "RWCT technology in Russian language and literature classes", the students were offered to apply theoretical knowledge in practice: to develop RWCT techniques when studying the story "Black Coat" by L.S. Petrushevskaya and analyze the proposed stages of the lesson:

Introductory speech of the teacher about L.S. Petrushevskaya with demonstration of the presentation.

Commented reading with characterization of the characters. Reading of Part 1.

Reading Part 2. Unexpected acquaintance (truck driver, man in the cab).

Reading 3 parts. Objects in the pocket of the girl's coat: matches, a piece of paper, a key. Where did the girl arrive? How did you see the train station? The houses?

Reading Part 4. What seemed creepy to the girl? What about you?

Part 5 reading. "A black coat saves from all troubles." How do you see the woman with the match?

Reading Part 6. What and how did the girl remember?

Reading Part 7. Why do you think the author showed us the "coming out of the nightmare" scene in the story? What does her conversation with her mother add to your opinion of the girl?

Reflection. Five-minute writing - answer to the question: "Does suicide save from all troubles, from solving problems?"

As a result, in the course of collective, group, pair and individual work the techniques "Synquain", "Diamant", "Thin and thick questions", "Ranking", "POPS - formula" were developed. We offer a theoretical and practical description of the listed techniques on the story "Black Coat" by L. Petrushevskaya.

SYNCWAY

The French word "cenqueme" means "fifth, five". A synquain is a five-line poem that requires synthesizing information and material in concise terms; in it, the author expresses his or her attitude to a problem. Writing a synquain develops an important skill - the ability to summarize information, to put complex feelings and ideas into a few words; it requires thoughtful reflection based on a rich vocabulary. Writing Rules:

1 line	Who? What?	One noun
Line 2	Which one? Which one? Which one? What kind?	Two adjectives
Line 3	Doing what? Doing what?	Three verbs
Line 4	The author's attitude toward the topic.	Four-word phrase
Line 5	Who? What?	One noun

"Synquain."

Hopelessness	A girl
Full, scary.	Frightened, lost
Torturing, crushing, suffocating	Walking, driving, remembering
In the trap of circumstance, a light is seen	On the edge of reality and nothingness
Wake up	Saved

DIAMANTE TECHNIQUE

Diamanta, a verse form of seven lines, the first and last of which are concepts with opposite meanings, is useful for working with concepts opposite in meaning. Description:

1 , **line 7** - antonymous nouns;

2 - two adjectives to the first noun;

3 - three verbs to the first noun;

4 - two noun phrases;

5 - three verbs to the second noun;

6 - two adjectives to the second noun.

"Diamante."

Death	Life
Imminent, premature.	A fleeting, valuable
Giving, silent, depriving.	Joyful, fulfilling, moving
The endless night, the eternal cold	Gives surprises, makes a decision
Deprives, rages, bestows	Scares you, takes you away, calms you down.

Bright colors, all kinds of sounds.	"Solves problems," a sense of injustice
Life	Death

THE "THICK AND THIN QUESTIONS" TECHNIQUE

Thick and thin questions are used to organize mutual questioning. A thin question presupposes an unambiguous short answer. A thick question implies an extended answer. After studying a topic, students are asked to formulate three "thin" and three "thick" questions" related to the material covered. Learners then question each other using the thick and thin questions tables. Examples of **"thick"** questions might include the following: Give three explanations why...? Explain why...? Why do you think...? Why do you think.? What is the difference.? What would happen if..? What if? Was there? Do you agree? Is it true? Examples of **"subtle"** questions: Who? What? When? Can.? Will? Could.? What is the name of...?

Subtle issues

Who is the author of the story "The Black Coat"? Who is the main character in the story "The Black Coat"? When does the event take place? Do the characters have names? What happened to the girl in the black coat? Who did the girl meet with? Could the girl have stayed there?

Thick questions

Explain why the girl is in this situation. Explain why the author uses black and white colors? Do you agree with the author who brought the girl back to the real world? Did the heroines of the story do the right thing?

RANKING TECHNIQUE

"Ranking" (from the French gapdeg - to build) - a technique in which the student arranges all the objects in the list in a row in ascending or descending order, significance or importance, etc. of a given criterion. The "Ranking" technique helps learners to analyze and evaluate the elements of the object, to define and specify their criteria for selection, to argue the selected options, to consider and compare arguments "for" and "against", to consider issues from different points of view.

What's important to me?

Life, tranquility, love, stability, happiness, peace, well-being, health, family.

What's important to a girl?

To warm up, to run away, to find, to remember, to return, to love, to die, to forget.

MATCHMAKING

When using the "Matching" technique, students are required to match a word or expression to a proposed description; this is a good technique for reinforcing the meaning of concepts.

Black coat.	Kids, I love you
As long as the match is lit	and felt sorry for her.
I don't want to do that anymore,	Saves you from all
Someone stood quietly in front of her.	You can still save yourself

"POPS FORMULA" TECHNIQUE

The PRES-formula technique was created by law professor David McCoyd Mason from South Africa. PRES-formula- Position-Reason- Explanation or Example-Summary means "Position, Reason, Example, Consequence". The value of this technique is that it allows students to briefly express their own position on the topic studied. A short statement in accordance with the PSS-formula consists of four elements:

P - position (what is the point of view)	I believe (believe) that ...
O - justification (argument in support of a position)	... because ... because.
P - example (facts that illustrate the argument)	... for example .for example......
C - consequence (conclusion)	... therefore ... thus

POPS -formula on the topic: "Did the girl do the right thing by committing suicide?"

П	I think the girl was reckless in her decision to commit suicide.
О	Because that decision could have led to other misfortunes.
П	For example, the death of an unborn child, illness and the experiences of loved ones.
C	And that's why you can't make tough decisions in moments of despair, anger.

Thus, the use of critical thinking technology in the teaching and learning process helps to increase interest in both the material being studied and the learning process itself; the ability to think critically and responsibly about one's own education; the ability to work in collaboration with others; and to improve the quality of education.

LITERATURE

1.   Diane Halpern. The Psychology of Critical Thinking. - St. Petersburg, 2000.

2.   Janie Steele, Kurt Meredith, Charles Temple. Project: Reading and Writing for the Development of Critical Thinking // Training Manual. - Bishkek, 2000.

3.   Petrushevskaya L.S. Black Coat. - M., 2014.

Printed by Books on Demand GmbH, Norderstedt / Germany